Reflections

A collection of nature inspired poems
to ruminate and enlighten.

Deepti Shetty

BookLeaf
Publishing

India | USA | UK

Made with ❤ on the BookLeaf Publishing Platform
www.bookleafpub.in
www.bookleafpub.com

To my family—your unwavering support, endless love, and boundless encouragement have been the foundation of this journey. This book is as much yours as it is mine.

Dad, your wisdom, strength, and belief in me have been guiding lights through every chapter of my life. This book is a testament to the values you've instilled in me and the dreams you've helped me chase. Thank you for always being my rock and inspiration. Miss you!

Acknowledgement

I would like to acknowledge the love and support of my family and friends, who have encouraged me to share my words with the world.

Preface

As we navigate the complexities of modern life, it's easy to lose sight of the world around us. The hustle and bustle of daily routines can leave us feeling disconnected from the natural world and from each other. But the truth is, we are not separate entities – we are part of a delicate web of life, connected by invisible threads that weave us into the fabric of the earth.

In this collection of poems, I invite you to reflect on the beauty of connection that surrounds us. Through the lens of nature, I explore the intricate relationships between the natural world and our own human experiences. I encourage you to slow down, look closely, and find hope in everyday things.

These poems are not just about the world outside – they are also about the world within. They are about the whispers of our own hearts, the rhythms of our own souls, and the way we are all intertwined. As you read through these pages, I hope you will find yourself drawn into the beauty of the natural world and are reminded of the profound connections that bind us all. The poems in this collection are not meant to be a source of answers, but rather a catalyst for questions. For it is not the grand or the extraordinary that holds the greatest power – it is the small, the simple, and the ordinary that reminds us of our place in the world, and our connection to each other.

As you embark on this journey of reflection, I invite you to look deeper within, to see the world in a new light, and to find the beauty in the everyday. For in doing so, we may just find that the most profound truths are hidden in plain sight, waiting for us to notice.

1. Whispers From the Window

In the hushed dawn, where blue and gold embrace,

The world awakens, at a glacial pace.

The turbulent sky, a mirrored soul,

A reflection of the artist's deepest, darkest role.

The village sleeps, a quiet, expectant hush,

Cypress trees stand watch, like sentinels of
ancient rush.

Their branches stretch, like withered fingers,
towards the sky,

As if to guide the gaze, to the swirling clouds
that pass by.

As sunrise breaks, the shadows slowly recede,

The stars remain, like diamonds scattered, a
celestial seed.

The village below, a peaceful, serene nest,

A haven from the turmoil, that the artist's
heart has confessed.

In Starry Night, we glimpse the artist's inner
turmoil,

A reflection of his struggles, his thoughts in
pain that recoil.

A cry for solace, a cry for peace,

A cry to be heard, to be released, to cease.

The cypress trees, like dark, mysterious
guides,

Lead the eye, to the swirling clouds, where
emotions reside.

The swirling clouds, a symbol of his inner
strife,

A reminder that even in darkness, there is
always life, a glimmer of light.

As we gaze upon this masterpiece so fine,

We see a piece of the artist's soul, so divine.

A piece of himself, laid bare and true,

A piece of his heart, that beats for me, and for you.

In Starry Night, we find a sense of calm,

A sense of peace, that echoes through the storm.

A reminder that darkness will pass, and the light will cope,

And even in turmoil, there is always hope.

2. A Moment's Peace

As I step through the door, the day's weight
falls away,

A cup of coffee in hand, my weary soul's first
ray.

Of solace, a moment's peace, before the
world's loud din,

I seek refuge in familiar sounds, where heart
and mind can win.

My favorite song, a trusted friend, a calm for
my troubled mind,

A melody that whispers calm and leaves my
worries behind.

The notes begin to swirl, a gentle breeze that
stirs the air,

My shoulders relax, my heart beats slower, a
gentle prayer.

As I let the music wash over me, my thoughts
begin to unwind,

The tension eases, the stress subsides, and my
mind is left behind.

I breathe a little deeper, and my body starts
to sway,

The rhythm of the song, a soothing balm,
drives all my worries away.

In this fleeting moment, I am free, untethered
and light,

My cares and concerns, like autumn leaves,
drift away into the night.

I am reminded to take care, to prioritize my
mind's might,

To pause, to breathe, to let the music guide
me through the darkest night.

The song's refrain becomes a mantra, a
reminder to be kind,

To myself, to my soul, to the fragility of the
human mind.

I am not alone, I am not lost, I am not
without a friend,

For in the silence, and in the song, I find a
sense of peace that never ends.

So let us cherish these moments, these songs
that soothe and heal,

These reminders to take care, to breathe, to
let our souls reveal.

The beauty, the wonder, the hope that's
hidden deep inside,

For in music and silence, we find our truest
guide.

3. Hope Eternal

The seasons come and go, slow and steady,

Each one a reminder that change is always headed our way,

Summer's warmth fades away, and autumn's chill sets in,

Leaves fall, and the world starts to feel like it's giving in.

Winter's darkness is hard to bear,

Frosty mornings, and the world's asleep,
without a care,

But even in the cold, there's a spark,

A promise of new life, a chance to embark.

Come Spring, the days get longer, the nights
get shorter,

The earth starts to wake up, and new life is
born, no matter,

The sun starts to rise, and with it comes,

A sense of hope, and a new dawn's hum.

The seasons come and go, a cycle that's true,

Of growth and decay, of life anew,

And though the changes can be hard to face,

There's always hope, in every season's place.

Here comes the sun, with all its might,

Bringing light to banish the dark of the night,

And though the journey's long, and winding
too,

Hope remains, a beacon shining through.

So let the seasons turn, and bring their
change,

For in the end, the sun will still arrange,

A new beginning, a fresh start to make,

And hope will rise, in the morning's wake.

4. Windows to the Soul

The eyes, they say, reflect the soul,

A place where dreams and doubts unroll.

Each glance a portal to the mind,

Where every fear and hope we find.

In every look, a question lies,

A silent plea, a soft surprise.

The mirror shows what words can't say,

A glimpse of light in shades of gray.

For in the eyes, the truth we see,

Is all we are, and all we'll be.

5. The Beauty of Human Connection

The beauty of human connection, a bond so strong and true,

A friendship that's chosen, a family that's new,

Through life's ups and downs, we find our way,

And friends are there to guide us, night and day.

They're the ones who lift us up, when we're
feeling down,

Who put a smile on our face, and turn our
frown around,

They're the ones who listen, care and
understand,

And are always there, with a helping hand.

We may get busy, with our daily grind,

But one unplanned call, can turn our day
around,

A friend's voice on the line, a ray of sunshine
bright,

Can chase the blues away and make
everything alright.

Friends are the light of our lives, a precious gift indeed,

A treasure to be cherished, and a bond to be freed,

They're the ones who make us laugh, who make us cry,

Who are always there, to be by our side.

So, let's cherish these bonds, these ties that bind,

These friendships that bring us joy, and make our hearts and souls align,

For in the beauty of human connection, we find our way,

To a life of love, laughter, and joy each day.

6. Wings of Thought

Thoughts take flight on wings unseen,

Through skies of blue and fields of green.

They drift on winds, both wild and still,

Through distant lands, through heart and
will.

Each thought reflects a secret tune,

A rising sun, a fading moon.

It soars where only dreams may go,

Through endless realms we'll never know.

For in the mind, the skies are wide,

And thought is free, with wings untied.

7. Ophelia

I'll tell you about a time,

When I was a little girl,

The innocent world was all mine,

And yes, were all those curls.

The charms were all around,

Toys, candies, ribbons abound,

And yes, as sweet as I sound,

Happiness was here profound.

I was on this bus I tell,

What I saw, set my foot a fleet,

A plethora of flowers all so well,

Made my heart skip a beat.

So enamored was I with the flowers,

Pretty flowers in every hue,

The old man saw that I loved those flowers,

Violets, Blues, and Honeydew.

I was enchanted by the flowers' beauty rare,

The old man noticed, and his eyes showed he cared,

He told me they were for his wife, a tender gesture true,

But I wished I could ask, though I was shy, and couldn't do

With a smile on his face, he gave me those flowers,

Then I was giddy in a trance,

For them, he treaded his garden for hours,

But said, worry not, I'll give my wife assurance.

Then he got down from the bus and walked away,

And that's all I have to say,

For he walked through the cemetery door,

Where six feet under, his Ophelia lay.

8. A Calm Abode

A pool of water, calm and deep,

Holds within the dreams we keep.

It mirrors back the sky so wide,

And all the secrets we confide.

A single stone, when cast within,

Can stir the depths where thoughts begin.

Yet when the ripples fade away,

The stillness keeps the night at bay.

In that pool, we find the key,

The secrets to calmness till eternity.

9. A Pat on the Back

I remember the day I felt like I'd hit really
low,

My grades were bad, and my family got to
know.

I thought I'd let them down, and that I'd
never be okay,

I felt like I'd failed them, and that I'd never
find my way.

I walked home from school that day, feeling
lost and alone,

I couldn't think of anything, except for my
failures.

I felt like I was drowning, in a sea of despair,

I didn't know how to get out, or how to show
I cared.

My father walked back with me all along,

No words exchanged, yet his presence felt
strong.

He too was disappointed, seeing I was glum,

And then he patted my back and reassured,
we shall overcome.

That pat on the back, gave me a new start,

I worked hard to prove myself, to show my family that I care.

I studied every morning and night, and gave it my all,

And with every small success, my confidence grew, my fears started to fall.

Positive gestures can change everything, they can lift us up,

My dad's pat gave me the strength to turn things around, to never give up.

We all need a little bit of kindness, a little bit of love,

To make us feel like we're enough, like we're worthy of the stars above.

I learned that day, that it's okay to make
mistakes,

That it's okay to fall, and that we can always
get back up, and make our own way.

My dad's pat, his confidence in me, taught
me,

That with hard work and dedication, you can
overcome and be what you wish to be.

10. Echoes of Stillness

In the quiet lake, the sky bends low,

A mirror of clouds, in gentle glow.

The mountains bow, their peaks dissolve,

In waters deep, where secrets evolve.

The world reflects, a perfect twin,

Of what's without, and what's within.

Yet ripples stir, a silent fight,

Between the dark and morning light.

In stillness, we become the air,

A fleeting thought, a whispered prayer.

II. Moonlit Shadows

Beneath the moon's soft, silken gaze,

The night unveils its quiet maze.

The shadows dance, the stars reply,

In silver hues, the darkened sky.

We walk in silence, hand in hand,

Across the shore, the endless sand.

Each step a note, a fleeting sound,

Our echoes lost, yet ever found.

The moon reflects our whispered dreams,

In shadowed light and silver streams.

12. Beneath the Surface

What lies beneath the surface clear,

A world untouched by doubt or fear.

The waters hide a thousand tales,

Of fleeting fish and silver scales.

Our thoughts, like stones, sink deep below,

Into the depths where truth may grow.

Yet mirrored skies deceive the mind,

And leave the answers hard to find.

In waters deep, the soul will see,

Reflections of what is meant to be.

13. Winds of Time

The wind that stirs the autumn leaves,

Carries with it the past it grieves.

A thousand voices, soft and still,

Whisper through the forest's will.

Each branch, a memory of days,

Where shadows danced in sunlight's rays.

The wind reflects what once was clear,

A fleeting glimpse of yesteryear.

And though the leaves may fade and fall,

The winds of time remember all.

14. The Echoing Hills

The hills, they speak in echoes low,

Of winds that stir, of streams that flow.

Each voice reflects the earth's own song,

A melody both pure and strong.

The whispers climb to skies so wide,

And roll along the mountainside.

In every sound, a truth is told,

Of nature's heart, both young and old.

For in the hills, we hear the call,

Of something greater, after all.

15. Silent Conversations

The river speaks in whispered tones,

Of distant lands, of ancient stones.

Its voice, a song both fierce and kind,

A secret language of the mind.

It mirrors trees that line its way,

Reflecting skies at break of day.

But in its depths, where shadows swim,

The river's words grow dark and dim.

In silence, it invites us in,

To see the places, we've never been.

16. The Space Between

Between the stars, a quiet grace,

A hidden world, a sacred space.

The night reflects what light has shown,

Yet keeps the mysteries unknown.

In moments still, we feel the pull,

Of time, of love, of something full.

It's in the space where nothing lies,

We find the truth behind the skies.

For in the gaps, the silence hums,

The world, it speaks where nothing comes.

17. River of Dreams

A river flows through dreams untold,

Its waters clear, yet dark and cold.

It carries whispers from the past,

Of fleeting moments, gone so fast.

It winds through hills and valleys deep,

Through endless nights when stars still sleep.

It mirrors faces, skies, and stone,

Yet each reflection stands alone.

And though the river's course may bend,

Its journey never finds an end.

18. A Glass of Rain

A raindrop falls, crystal clear,

A fleeting trace of sky so near.

It lands on glass and softly stays,

A world reflected in its gaze.

The trees bend low, the clouds descend,

The raindrop holds them as a friend.

But soon it fades, its shape undone,

And leaves the glass to catch the sun.

In every drop, a world may lie,

But none are meant to last or fly.

19. The Unseen Thread

There's a thread that runs through night and day,

Invisible, but it lights the way.

It ties the stars, it binds the sea,

And stretches out through you and me.

Though often lost in light and sound,

It's in the quiet that it's found.

It links our hearts to distant skies,

And whispers truths behind our eyes.

The thread reflects all that we seek,

A bond so strong, yet soft and meek.

20. The Distant Flame

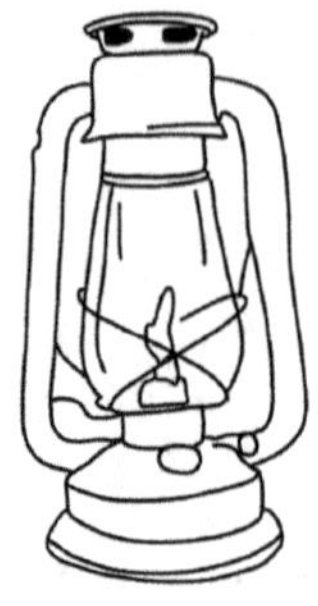

A candle flickers in the night,

Its flame a soft, eternal light.

It casts reflections on the wall,

Of shadows dancing, rising tall.

Though wind may blow, it never dies,

It holds the truth behind our eyes.

A single spark can warm the cold,

A fragile light that makes us bold.

And in its glow, we learn to see,

The flame within both you and me.

21. The Secret Life of a Leaf

In the tree's canopy, a leaf does abide,

A secret life, where the world outside does hide.

Like the veins that flow, and the edges that sway,

Our emotions ebb and flow, like the leaf's gentle way.

The leaf's voice, a rustling sound,

Echoes the whispers of our hearts profound.

In its beauty, we find our own inner peace,

A sense of calm, that the world can't release.

The leaf's gentle touch, a soothing balm to our soul,

Easing the pains, that make us whole.

In its fragile form, we find our own strength,

A resilience that helps us, to face life's length.

22. Aspirations

The mountain stands tall and strong,

A symbol of courage, where hearts belong.

Like the peaks that touch the sky,

Our dreams and aspirations never die.

The mountain's beauty, a treasure rare,

Just like our inner selves, beyond compare.

In its ruggedness, we find our might,

A reflection of our inner light.

The mountain's grandeur, a source of pride,

Where our spirits soar, and our hearts reside.

A reminder to stay still, when worlds collide,

A reminder to stand tall, and never divide.

23. Stories Unfold

The river flows, a winding stream,

A metaphor for life's endless dream.

Like its ever-changing currents, we roam,

Through joys and sorrows, we find our home.

The river's voice, a soothing melody,

Echoes the whispers of our hearts' symphony.

In its depths, we find our own reflection,

A mirror to our soul's contemplation.

The river's journey, a path we all must take,

Where every step forward, our spirits make,

And with each bend, our stories unfold,

And the beauty of life, forever to behold.

24. Ocean's Embrace

The ocean's vastness, a mystery to share,

A symbol of the depths of our own care.

Like its waves that crash, and its tides that rise,

Our emotions ebb and flow, like the ocean's sighs.

The ocean's roar, a thunderous voice,

A reminder of our own inner choice.

In its depths, we find our own inner space,

A sanctuary to heal and find our own pace.

The ocean's beauty, a treasure to behold,

Where our spirits find solace, and our hearts
unfold,

And with each wave, our fears are washed
away,

And the horizon's promise, brings a brighter
day.

25. Forest of Dreams

The forest whispers secrets, of the past and present,

A symbol of our own inner wisdom, and its consent.

Like its trees that stand, and its leaves that sway,

Our thoughts and feelings, in a perpetual way.

The forest's silence, a stillness to hear,

A reminder of our own inner voice, so clear.

In its shadows, we find our own inner light,

A guiding force, that shines through the
night.

In its openness, we find our own space,

A freedom to roam, and a joyous pace.

The forest's magic, a world to explore,

Where our dreams and imagination, forever
roar.

26. A Sunset to Remember

The sunset's warmth, a gentle, golden light,

A symbol of hope, and a peaceful night.

Like its hues that fade, and its stars that shine,

Our dreams and aspirations, forever divine.

The sunset's beauty, a treasure to see,

A reminder of the beauty, that's meant to be.

In its glow, we find our own inner peace,

A sense of calm, that the world can't release.

The sunset's magic, a world to explore,

Where our spirits soar, and our hearts are free
once more.

With every sunset, we're reminded to dream,

And the stars' soft whisper, a gentle, loving
theme.

27. A Storm Within

The storm's intensity, a force to be told,

A symbol of strength, and a story to unfold.

Like its winds that howl, and its rains that
pour,

Our passions and desires, forever in store.

The storm's power, a reminder of our own
might,

A symbol of resilience, and a will to fight.

In its darkness, we find our own inner light,

A guiding force, that shines through the
night.

The storm within, a treasure to behold,

Where our spirits are tested, and our hearts
are made bold.

With every storm, we're reminded to stand,

And the rainbow's promise, a brighter day at
hand.

28. Wildflowers

In a field of wildflowers, which no one did sow,

A beauty blooms that only nature can grow.

A symbol of freedom, in a world so free,

A reminder that life's beauty, is meant to be.

Like the petals that dance, in the breeze's
gentle sway,

Our joys and sorrows, forever intertwined in
play.

No gardener's care, no human hand did shape,

This wildflower field, a nature-created escape.

A wildflower's elegance, a treasure to behold,

A reminder of the beauty, that's meant to
unfold.

In its simplicity, we find our own inner peace,

A sense of wonder, that the world can't
release.

With every bloom, we're reminded to dream,

Under the sun's warm whisper, a gentle,
loving theme.

No walls or fences, can contain its might,

This field of wildflowers, a nature-created
delight.

29. A Tree's Wisdom

The tree's wisdom, an ancient, gentle soul,

A symbol of strength, and a story to unfold.

Like its branches that stretch, and its roots
that grow,

Our experiences and wisdom, forever in tow.

The tree's beauty, a treasure to behold,

A reminder of the charm, that's meant to be.

In its stillness, we find our own inner peace,

A sense of calm, that the world can't release.

The tree's magic, a world to explore,

Where our spirits soar, and our hearts are free
once more.

With every tree, we're reminded to stand,

And the wind's gentle whisper, a gentle,
loving hand.

30. An Ode to Mumbai

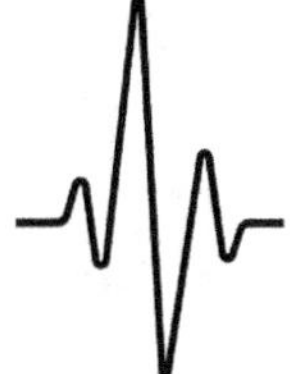

As I grew up in the bustling streets of
Mumbai,

I saw the city's resilience, its unbreakable
might.

A city born of chaos, yet it stands tall,

A testament to the human spirit, that never
falls.

I remember the sounds, the smells, the sights,

The cacophony of life, that never takes flight.

The city's imperfections, its rough edges too,

Make it beautiful, in a way that's uniquely
true.

I think of the people, who call this city home,

Their struggles, their triumphs, their stories
untold.

The way they adapt, the way they thrive,

In the face of adversity, they never say die.

I see it in the street vendors, who sell their
wares,

In the fishermen, who brave the rough seas
and dares.

I see it in the families, who live in small
spaces,

But find joy in the little things, with love in
their faces.

As I look back, I realize it's not just the city,

That's resilient, it's the people who are
Mumbai's heartbeat,

Their spirit is contagious, it spreads like a fire,

And inspires us to be brave, to never retire.

31. A Dream called Japan

Land of the rising sun, a dream within my sight,

A place of ancient wonder, where tradition meets delight,

I long to wander through the bamboo forest's gentle sway,

And marvel at the beauty of Arashiyama on a misty day.

I yearn to visit Fushimi Shrine, where sacred torii gates abide,

And Kinkakuji Temple's golden glow, fills my
heart and soul inside,

The valour of Himeji Castle's walls, a
testament to history's might,

And Mount Fuji's majestic peak, a symbol of
beauty and light.

And Itsukushima Shrine, a floating torii, a
sight to behold,

A place where spirituality and divinity,
beautifully unfold,

My lifelong dream, a journey to this land of
ancient charm,

Yearning to see the tradition, beauty, and
calm.

I long to stroll through Kyoto's by-lanes,
where secrets and stories unfold,

And find my inner zen in Kenrokuen
Garden's tranquil, serene hold,

I dream of moments of peace, surrounded by
monkeys' gentle play,

In Jigokudani's snowy wonderland, on a
winter's day.

But Tokyo's glitz and modern wonderland,
leaves me spellbound and aglow,

A city that never sleeps, where neon lights
dance and glow,

From Shibuya's famous scramble crossing to
Harajuku's fashion flair,

Tokyo's energy is infectious, and its modern
wonder, beyond compare.

32. The Quiet Sea

The ocean hums a song so low,

A melody the heart may know.

In every wave, a secret hides,

In every crest, the truth abides.

The moon reflects on waters still,

And stirs the depth with gentle will.

The tides, they rise, then softly fall,

Like echoes in a distant hall.

In silence, the sea speaks to my heart,

Of all we can be, a brand-new start.

In its depths, a wisdom lies in wait,

A reflection of our own inner state.

33. A Flicker of Dawn

A flicker of dawn on the horizon's edge,

A promise wrapped in gold, orange, and red.

The stars retreat, the night lets go,

Of dreams it whispered, soft and slow.

The sky reflects a waking light,

As shadows fade, embracing bright.

In every ray, a story begins,

Of hope reborn where night rescinds.

The morning hums a quiet song,

That leads us back where we belong.

In its gentle warmth, we find our way,

And the day's possibilities start to sway.

34. Grains of Sand

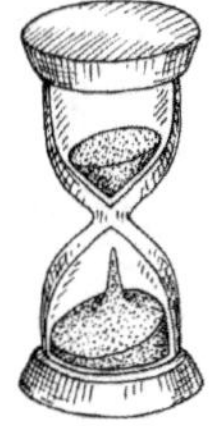

Grains of sand fall one by one,

In the hourglass, under the sun.

Each moment slips through unseen hands,

A fleeting trace on endless sands.

Time reflects what once has been,

A tapestry of loss and win.

Yet in its flow, we find our way,

A path that's carved from night till day.

For though the sands may fall and fade,

In their descent, the future's made.

In every grain, a story's told,

Of moments lived, and memories to hold.

35. The Hidden Path

Beneath the leaves, a path is laid,

Through forests deep, in quiet shade.

It twists and turns where light is dim,

A secret trail, serene and grim.

Each step we take, a choice we make,

In silent woods where hearts may ache.

Yet in the dark, reflections gleam,

Of what we are, and what we dream.

84

For every road, though veiled and long,

Leads somewhere we have known all along.

And though the journey may be hard to find,

The path ahead, a mystery to unwind.

36. A Babbling Brook

A babbling brook, a gentle stream,

A symbol of peace, and a soothing dream.

Like its waters that flow, and its banks that bend,

Our emotions ebb and flow, like the brook's gentle trend.

The brook's voice, a calming melody,

Echoes the whispers of our hearts' symphony.

In its depths, we find our own reflection,

A mirror to our soul's contemplation.

The brook's journey, a path we all must take,

Where every step forward, our spirits make.

With every ripple, we're reminded to flow,

And the brook's gentle song, a peaceful heart
does grow.

37. A Candle's Flame

A candle's flame, a warm and gentle light,

A symbol of hope, and a guiding sight.

Like its sparks that dance, and its warmth
that spreads,

Our passions and desires, forever in our
heads.

The flame's roar, a soothing voice,

Echoes the whispers of our hearts' choice.

In its warmth, we find our own inner peace,

A sense of calm, that the world can't release.

The flame's magic, a world to explore,

Where our spirits soar, and our hearts are free
once more.

With every flicker, we're reminded to dream,

And in the flame's gentle warmth, a loving
heart does beam.

38. Finding Monet in Giverny

Monet's garden, a vibrant and colorful sight,

A symbol of beauty, and a joyous delight.

Like its peonies that bloom, and willows that sway,

Our joys and sorrows, forever in play.

The garden's voice, a symphony of sound,

Echoes the whispers of our hearts profound.

In its beauty, we find our own inner peace,

A sense of wonder, that the world can't
release.

The garden's magic, a world to explore,

Where our spirits soar, and our hearts are free
once more.

With every bloom, we're reminded to grow,

And the garden's vibrant colors, a joyful heart
does show.

As spring arrives, the tamaris trees come
alive,

Their delicate flowers, a gentle, sweet
surprise.

The irises bloom, in hues of purple and blue,

A majestic beauty, that's both strong and true.

The lupins stand tall, with their spiky,
colorful might,

A symbol of resilience, in the face of night.

And when summer's warmth, brings life to
the land,

The ginkgo trees, with their bright green
leaves, take stand.

In this vibrant tapestry, of colors and sound,

We find our own reflection, in the beauty all
around.

A sense of connection, to the natural world
outside,

A reminder to cherish, the beauty that we
can't hide.

For in Monet's garden, we find our own
peaceful nest,

A place to rest, and let our spirits find their
best.

A symbol of hope, and joy, and love, and
light,

A reminder to cherish, the beauty of life's
delight.

39. Jardin Botaniques at Geneva

In Jardin Botaniques, at Geneva's heart,

A world of beauty, a work of art.

Like the flowers that bloom, and the trees
that stand,

Our hopes and dreams, forever in demand.

The garden's voice, a symphony of sound,

Echoes the whispers of our hearts profound.

In its beauty, we find our own inner peace,

A sense of wonder, that the world can't
release.

The garden's magic, a world to explore,

Where our spirits soar, and our hearts are free
once more.

With every bloom, we're reminded to grow,

And the garden's vibrant colors, a joyful heart
does show.

But little did I know, on that summer's day,

I was searching for solace, in a world gone
astray.

Internal turmoil, a stormy sea,

Had taken its toll, on my heart and me.

I sought refuge, in this garden so fair,

A place of peace, where love and beauty share.

And then I saw, a tiny gate,

That led to a world, beyond my fate.

A black gate, with no handle to hold,

But a glimpse of blue, that beckoned me to
unfold.

I took a step, and removed my shoe,

And let my feet, touch the cool blue dew.

The water's chill, was like a balm to my soul,

And my pains, began to fade, like a waning
roll.

The blue water, glistened in the sun's warm
light,

And I felt my heart, begin to take flight.

The world outside, with all its strife,

Seemed distant, as I stood in this peaceful life.

The garden's magic, had worked its spell,

And I was healed, in that moment, all was
well.

40. Allure of the Willows

By the river's edge, the willows sway,

A gentle dance, in the breeze's gentle way.

Like the branches that bend, and the leaves that play,

Our emotions ebb and flow, like the river's gentle bay.

The willow's voice, a soothing melody,

Echoes the whispers of our hearts' symphony.

In its beauty, we find our own inner peace,

A sense of calm, that the world can't release.

98

The willow's magic, a world to explore,

Where our spirits soar, and our hearts are free
once more.

With every sway, we're reminded to bend,

And the willow's gentle strength, a heart does
amend.

41. New Horizons Ahead

A new start, a fresh chance, a blank page to
fill,

A time to leave the past behind, and a dream
to build,

The possibilities are endless, but there's a fear
to begin,

A chance to find a new path, and a new sense
of purpose within.

The gift of new beginnings, a reminder to
take a breath,

To believe in yourself, and your abilities, and
have faith in your strength,

To take the leap, and let go of fear's tight grip,

And trust that you'll find your way, and learn
to navigate the trip.

With every new start, comes a chance to learn
and grow,

To make mistakes, and find a new way to go,

To discover new strengths, and uncover
hidden depths,

To find a new sense of purpose, and a new
rhythm to keep.

The gift of new beginnings, a reminder to stay true,

To yourself, and your dreams, and all that you pursue,

To keep faith in yourself, and your abilities too,

To know that you are capable, and that you can see it through.

So take the leap, and let go of fear's tight grip,

And let the gift of new beginnings, be your guiding ship,

For in its promise, you'll find hope and renewal's might,

And a chance to start anew, and shine with all your light.